Cheap Licks

Cheap Licks
Cheap Licks
Cheap Licks
Cheap Licks
Cheap Licks
Cheap Licks

T0055945

To access video visit:
www.halleonard.com/mylibrary

Enter Code
6798-0846-5479-8733

Video Production by CI Design & DV Productions

Book Edited by Chad Johnson

Cover photo by Mike Graham

ISBN 978-1-5400-3848-7

HAL•LEONARD®

Visit Hal Leonard Online at
www.halleonard.com

Contact us:
Hal Leonard
7777 West Bluemound Road
Milwaukee, WI 53213
Email: info@halleonard.com

In Europe, contact:
Hal Leonard Europe Limited
42 Wigmore Street
Marylebone, London, W1U 2RN
il: info@halleonardeurope.com

In Australia, contact:
Hal Leonard Australia Pty. Ltd.
4 Lentara Court
Cheltenham, Victoria, 3192 Australia
Email: info@halleonard.com.au

CONTENTS

About the Video

All of the music examples in this book include video demos, so you can see and hear how they are played. Be sure to also check out Rick Nielsen's supplemental videos in which the man himself gives his own take on many of these ideas and musical concepts. You'll also hear plenty of great stories about Rick's influences and musical collaborations over the years. And, of course, many treasured guitars from his world-famous collection will be proudly on display as well!

Visit **www.halleonard.com/mylibrary** and enter the code from page 1 of this book to download or stream all the videos.

CHEAP LICKS ▶ INTRO

Great guitar solos don't have to be complicated; you can do a whole lot more with a few notes and some attitude than you might think! In this section, we're going to take a look at some ways to get the most we can from even the most modest of materials.

Early Rock 'n' Roll Style ▶ IN THE BEGINNING

Players like T-Bone Walker and Chuck Berry laid a pretty extensive framework for what would become known as "rock guitar," and much can be learned by familiarizing yourself with their legacy. In other words: If it ain't broke, don't fix it!

They both worked out of the minor pentatonic box form a good deal of the time. If you're not familiar with the shape, here's what it looks like in the key of A:

A Minor Pentatonic – Box Form

DEMO

5fr

Minor Pentatonic Staples

The following are must-know licks from this form. Notice that they're all slight variations on each other. We're playing three-note groupings: a bent note (fret 7 or 8) followed by two notes on fret 5 of strings 1 and 2.

DEMO

DEMO

You can repeat any of these licks for as long as you want! And, though we're working in the key of A here, this form is moveable since it doesn't contain any open strings. In other words, to play a B minor pentatonic scale, just move this form up two frets. To play a G minor pentatonic scale, just move it down two frets, etc.

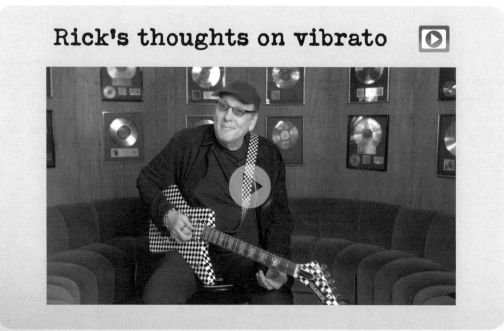

Rick's thoughts on vibrato

4

Building on the Foundation

You can use these "staple" licks as a foundation for creating other licks. Check out how each one is expanded into a fully formed lick:

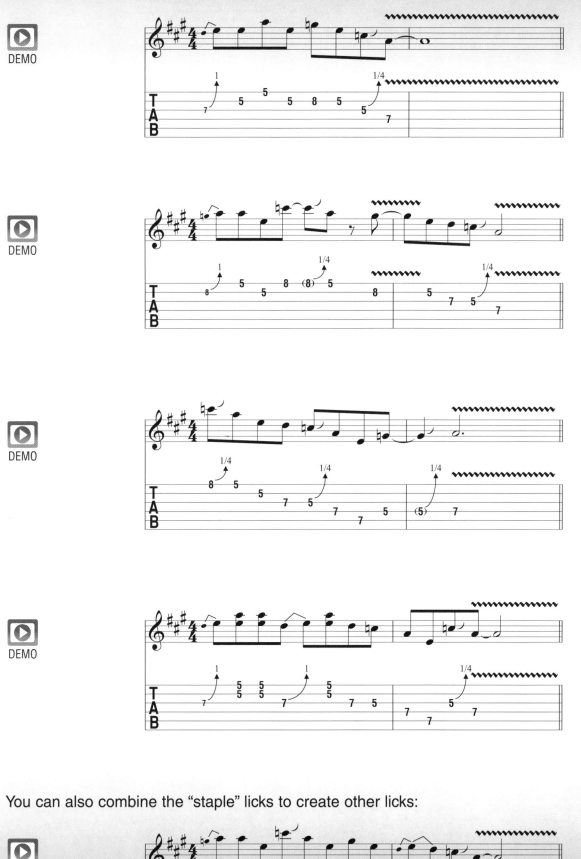

You can also combine the "staple" licks to create other licks:

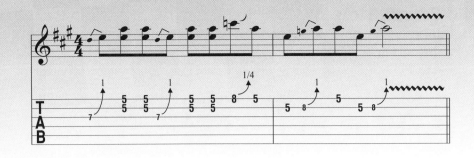

Adding Other Notes

Of course, you don't have to stick to only the minor pentatonic scale; you can add a few notes to this scale form to really open up the possibilities—something Chuck Berry and company would do quite often.

In the key of A, here's what a composite scale form looks like when you add some choice notes to the minor pentatonic form:

A Minor Pentatonic with Added Notes

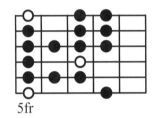

5fr

Don't worry about this scale's name—it doesn't really have one. Just know that it sounds great!

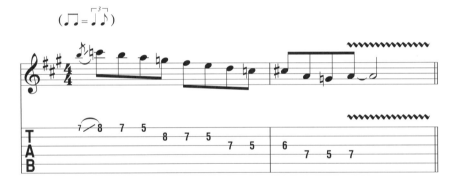

Extension Form

This is another very common form that's often connected with the standard box shape. In the key of A, it looks like this:

A Minor Pentatonic – Extension Form

DEMO

8fr

And here are a few ways you can use this form:

DEMO

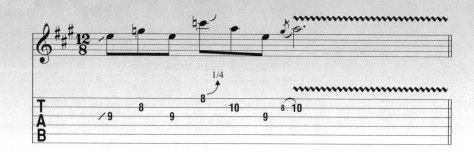

DEMO

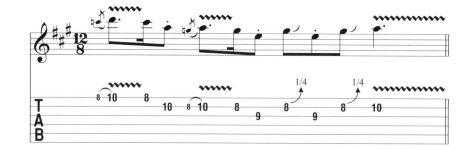

Bridging the Forms

It's also very common to bridge these two forms in one seamless lick:

DEMO

DEMO

DEMO

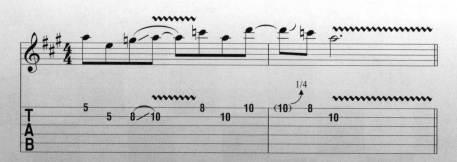

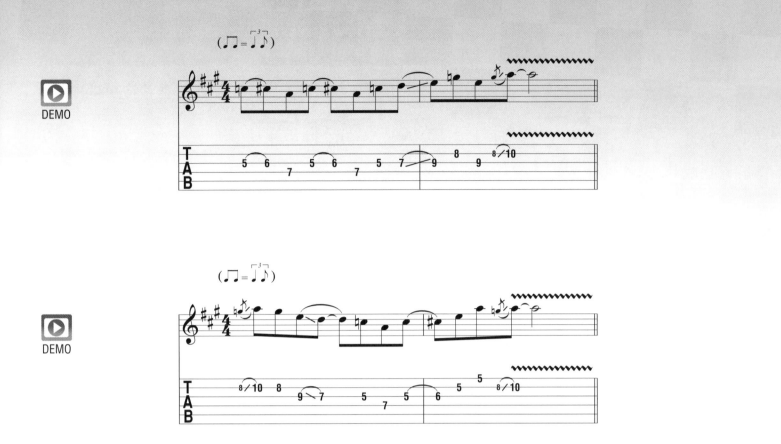

Double Stops

Another classic technique used in rock 'n' roll—from early to modern—is the *double stop*. In other words, you play two notes at one time. These notes are usually on adjacent strings in these licks, and you can create an almost limitless amount of licks from the forms we've already looked at.

Bend 'em, slide 'em… you name it!

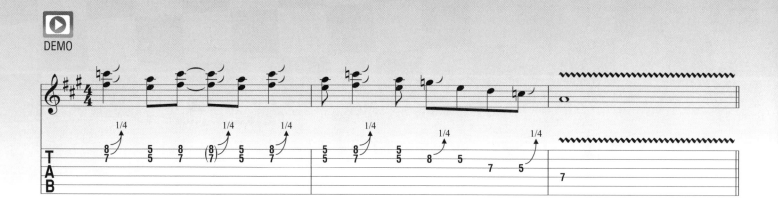

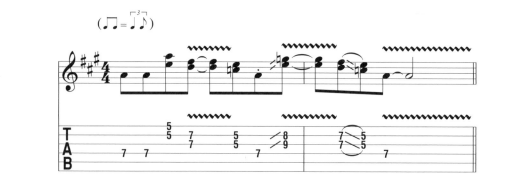

Country-Tinged Licks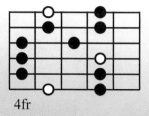

When you incorporate the *major pentatonic scale*, instead of just the minor pentatonic, you get more of a country rock sound.

Here's an A major pentatonic form based around fourth and fifth position:

A Major Pentatonic – Fourth Position

4fr

When you add some bends, slides, and hammer-ons/pull-offs to this form, you can get some great-sounding licks:

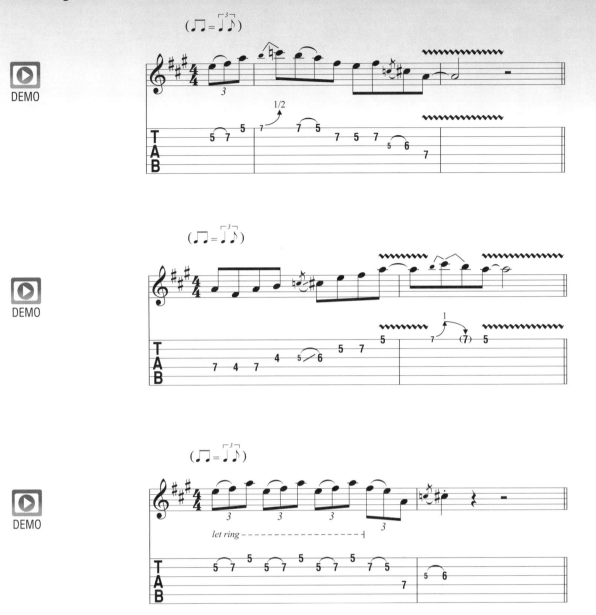

Another common form for A major pentatonic is up in ninth position. Though all six strings are shown, the top three strings are, by far, used the most.

A Major Pentatonic – Ninth Position

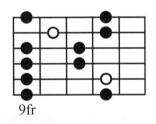

9fr

This form was B.B. King's favorite. Let's check out some licks…

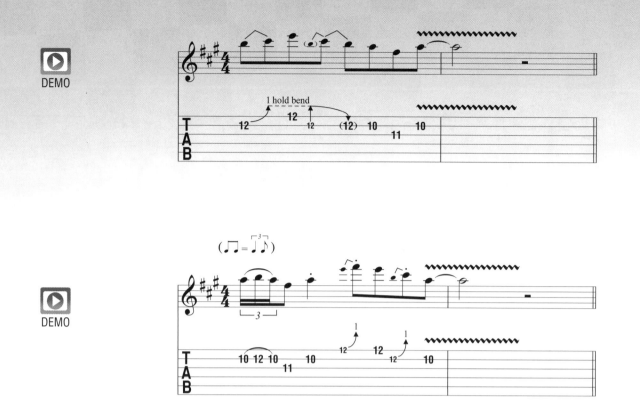

And finally, here's another common major pentatonic form. In the key of A, it's in second position:

A Major Pentatonic – Second Position

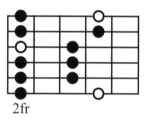

You may recognize that as the minor pentatonic box form we first learned on page 3. And you're right. But, in fifth position, it was an A minor pentatonic scale. In second position, it's A *major* pentatonic. This is sometimes called the "down three frets" trick. If you move a minor pentatonic scale form down three frets—from fifth position to second position, in the case of A minor pentatonic—you're now playing the *major* pentatonic scale in that key (A major pentatonic, in our case).

So, in this form you can play all those licks you learned from the minor pentatonic box form. The only difference is that you may need to resolve them differently because the tonic has changed. Compare this form to the one on page 3, and you can see how the tonics (the hollow circles in the diagrams) are in different spots.

Let's check out some licks in this form:

DEMO

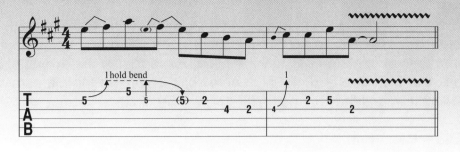

Here's a lick from the intro to "I Want You to Want Me" that uses this same form, only up an octave (in 14th position).

A Major Pentatonic – 14th Position

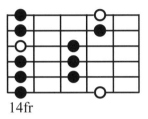

14fr

I Want You to Want Me – Major Pentatonic

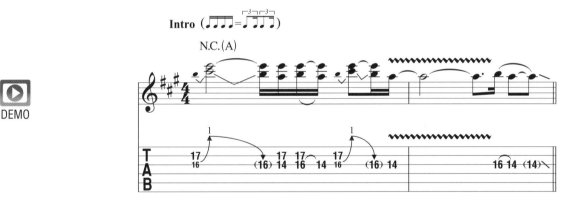

DEMO

Combining Major and Minor Pentatonic

Much of the allure of rock 'n' roll actually comes from the minor/major rub. In other words, major and minor tonalities are often combined to create that characteristic bluesy sound that's so prevalent in rock. You hear this in chords, melodies, solos, bass lines… you name it. It's a big part of the style.

So, how is this done with regard to playing licks? Well, simply put, we can combine major and minor pentatonic scales to get a whole new set of licks. We dabbled with this idea in the "Adding Other Notes" section on page 6, but now we'll explore it a bit more deeply.

A Quick Detour

Before we get to the mixing, though, we're going to do one more thing: we're going to turn our minor pentatonic forms into *blues scales*. To do this, we just need to add one note: the ♭5th. So far, we've looked at two different minor pentatonic forms: the main box form and the extended position. Now let's see what those look like when we add the "blue note," or the ♭5th. In the diagrams, the tonics (the A notes) will again be hollow, and the ♭5th notes (E♭/D♯) will be circled.

A Minor Pentatonic – Box Form

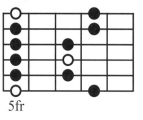

A Blues Scale – Box Form

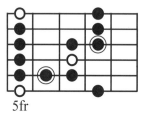

A Minor Pentatonic – Extension Form

8fr

A Blues Scale – Extension Form

8fr

Now let's take a look at some blues scale licks with these forms:

14

Tallying the Forms

Now let's take a look at all the pentatonic forms we've learned thus far (we'll add one more, too) in the key of A, both major and minor. Since the minor pentatonic is included in the blues scale—in other words, the blues scale is just the minor pentatonic with an added note—we'll just look at A major pentatonic and the A blues scale.

A Blues Scale, Box Form – Fifth Position

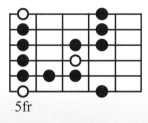

5fr

A Blues Scale, Extension Form – Eighth Position

8fr

And while we're at it, let's add one more common A blues form:

A Blues Scale – 12th Position

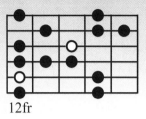

12fr

A Major Pentatonic – Second Position

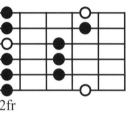

2fr

A Major Pentatonic – Fourth Position

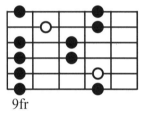

4fr

A Major Pentatonic – Ninth Position

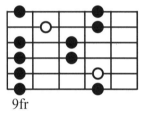

9fr

Spend some time playing through all of these forms, always being aware of where the tonic (A) is located. The tonic notes are always represented by the hollow circle on the scale diagrams.

Mixing It Up

OK, now that you have all these scale forms under your fingers, let's look at how we can combine them to create some licks. There's really no magic formula here; you kind of just learn what works for you through experience. In other words, there are different approaches to mixing the scales. Here are a few different approaches to get you started:

1. Try starting with A major pentatonic for the first half of a lick and then switch to A minor pentatonic/blues for the second half (or vice versa).

2. Try playing a lick entirely in A major pentatonic except for one note, which can come from A minor pentatonic/blues. Do the same the other way, as well.

3. Try using the notes from A major pentatonic on one string and the notes from A minor pentatonic/blues on the next string, etc.

4. Alternate between the scales every two notes, every three notes, every four notes, etc.

By using the previous approaches, along with the numerous scale forms at your disposal, you can create an almost limitless number of licks. (And remember that, though we're working in the key of A, you can transpose these licks to any other key just by moving them up or down the neck!) Let's check out some examples. We'll start in the fourth/fifth position area.

DEMO

DEMO

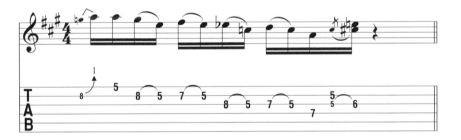

DEMO

Now let's move up a bit and mix the eighth-position A blues form with the ninth-position A major pentatonic form.

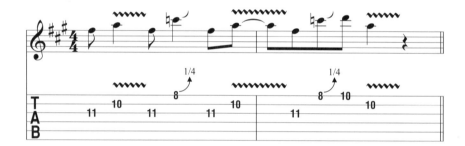

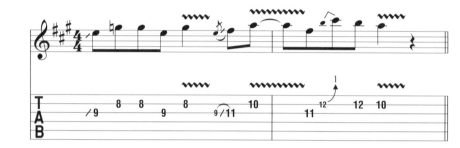

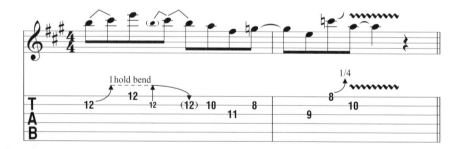

And here's the ninth-position A major pentatonic combined with the 12th-position A minor pentatonic/blues:

DEMO

DEMO

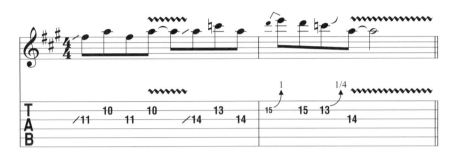

DEMO

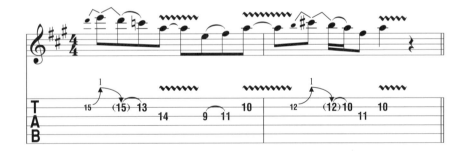

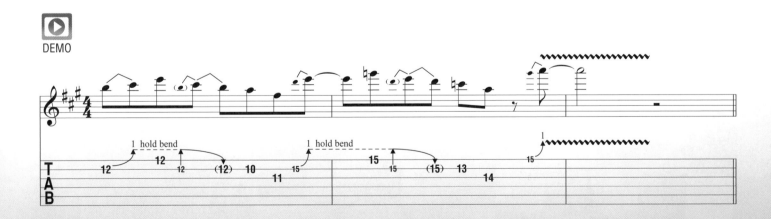

And now let's wander through all the forms!

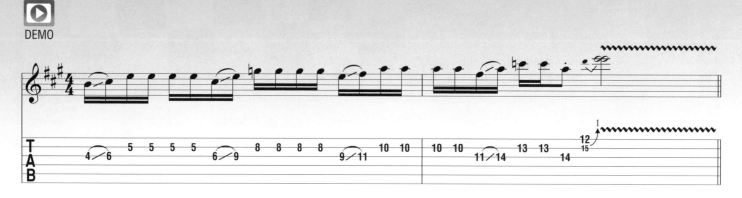

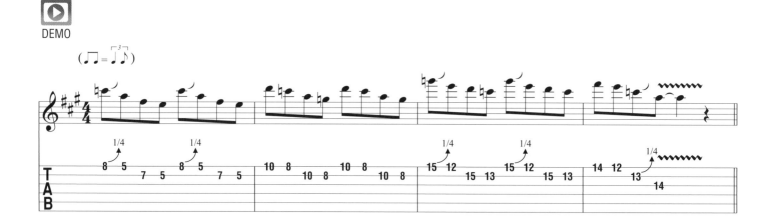

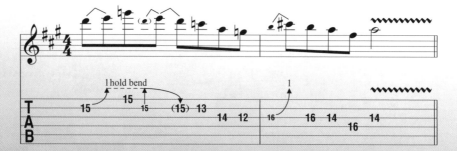

20

Rick's thoughts on harmonics

Flashy Hammer-On/Pull-Off Licks

If you want to inject a bit of excitement into a solo, you should never underestimate a well-placed, flashy legato lick. The term *legato*, which literally means "smooth and connected," refers to the use of hammer-ons and pull-offs (and sometimes slides) on guitar. From Jimi Hendrix and Jimmy Page to Chet Atkins and Albert Lee, countless players have exploited these types of licks for decades.

The Simple Hammer-Pull

Perhaps the most basic flashy lick consists of a four-note grouping. Three notes are played legato on a higher string, and one note is picked on a lower string, like this:

When you consider the different note choices and rhythmic possibilities, the variations are many. Here are a few classic moves from the A minor pentatonic/blues box shape:

DEMO

The order can be changed, too. You can have the hammer/pull portion at the end.

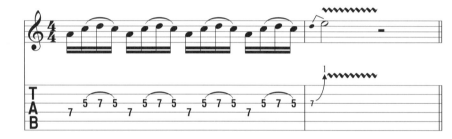

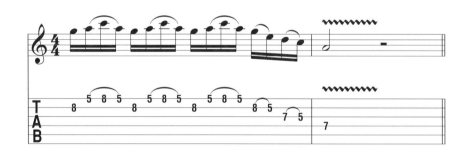

Or, you can mix them up:

DEMO

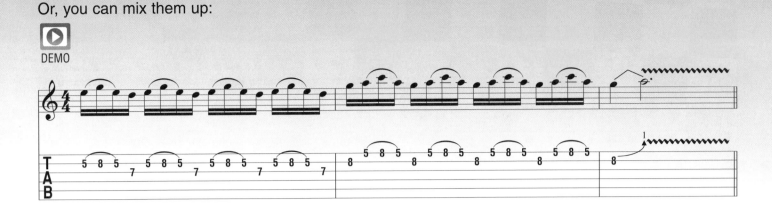

DEMO

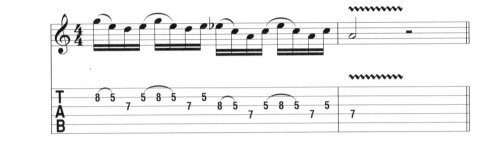

When you move the same idea up through different scale forms, it's an instant climax!

DEMO

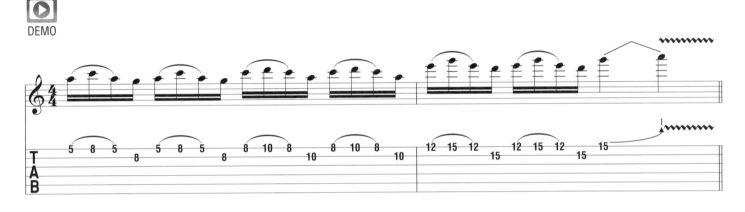

This next one passes through one minor pentatonic/blues form we haven't looked at yet. In A blues, it's based around ninth and 10th position:

A Blues Scale – Ninth Position

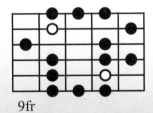

9fr

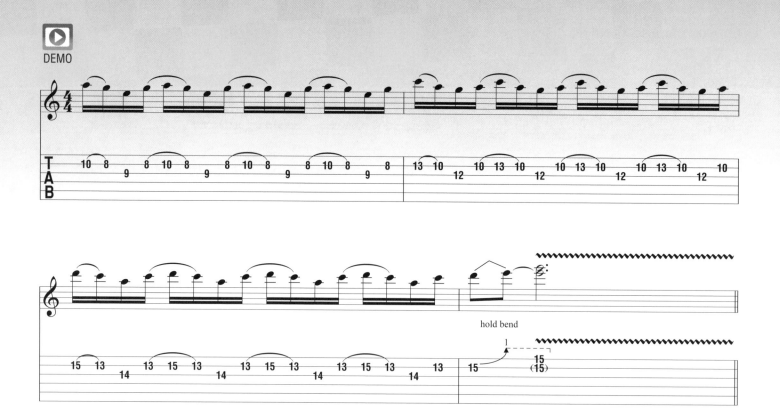

Or, you can move up through the strings within the same scale form.

A Blues Scale – 12th Position

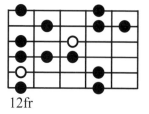

12fr

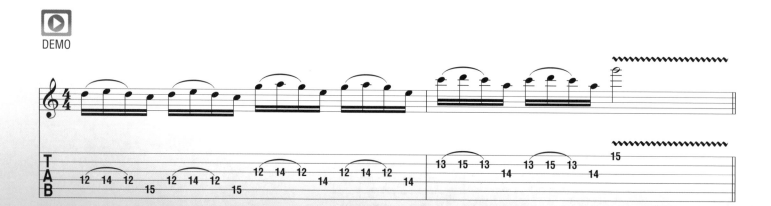

A Blues Scale – Fifth Position

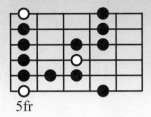

And of course, you can apply these same ideas to the major pentatonic scale, as well. Here are some examples with various A major pentatonic forms:

A Major Pentatonic – Fourth Position

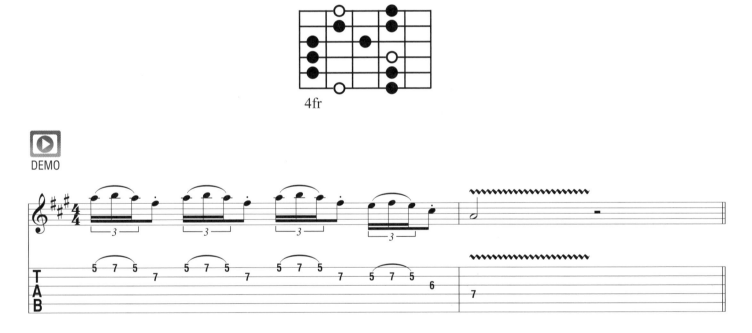

A Major Pentatonic – 14th Position

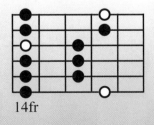

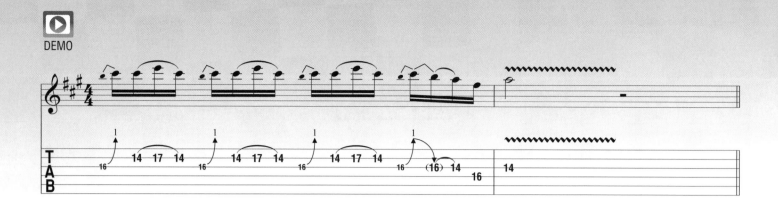

A Major Pentatonic – Ninth Position

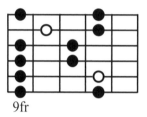

9fr

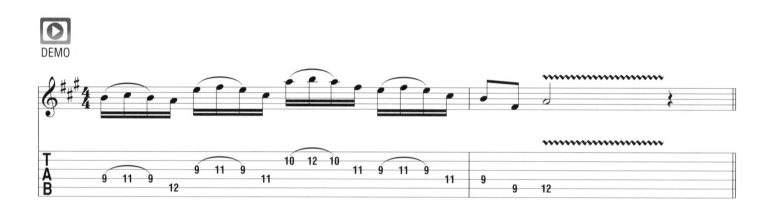

Don't forget that you can mix major pentatonic and minor pentatonic/blues, too! This one moves back and forth between A major pentatonic and A minor pentatonic.

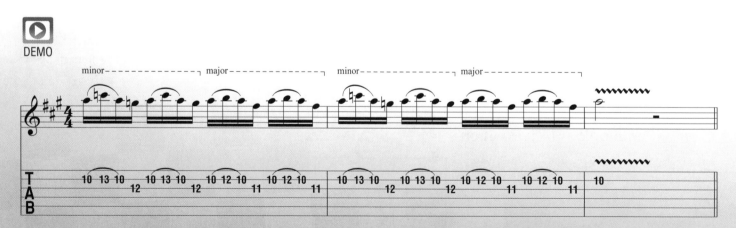

And this one is all A major pentatonic except for the C note at fret 8, which shows up every other beat.

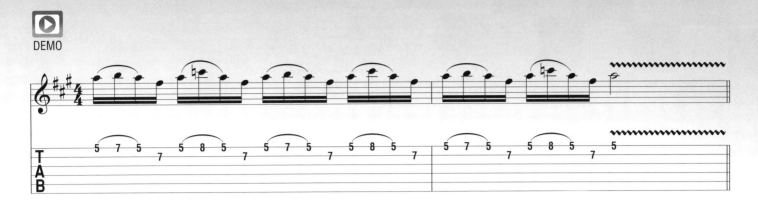

Open-String Pull-Offs

Another way to get some flash is to use open-string pull-offs. In these licks, you're usually playing two fretted notes and pulling them off to an open string, like this:

The big difference here is that, since we're using open strings, the licks will sound different, depending on what key you're in. They're used most often in C major or "sharp keys" like G, D, A, and E. But they'll still show up in other keys, as well.

SYMMETRICAL APPROACH

It's very common to use symmetrical fingerings for these licks—in other words, the same frets on each string throughout the lick. Keep in mind that it can be deceptively tricky to get these to sound super clean the way Chet Atkins would, for example. Start off slowly to make sure that all the notes are clean and even before you start speeding up.

Here's a classic lick in the key of G. You may notice that not all of these notes are technically in the key of G, but that's all right—it's the effect we're going for.

27

And here's one in A that's also very common:

This E minor lick is also a classic:

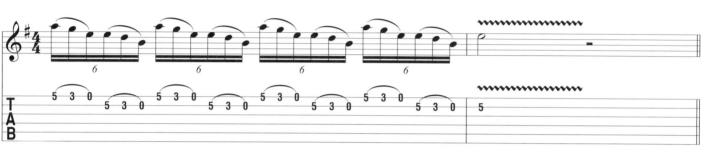

Here's how a symmetrical lick was used in "California Man." This is like the G lick we just learned, but this time it's played over an E chord for a different effect.

California Man – Pull-Offs

By simply altering a note in the shape, you can get something that works well in another key. For example, by moving the fifth-fret notes in the previous example up to fret 6, we get a lick that sounds great in G major (or G minor).

Move everything up one more fret, and we get a great one in the key of E major:

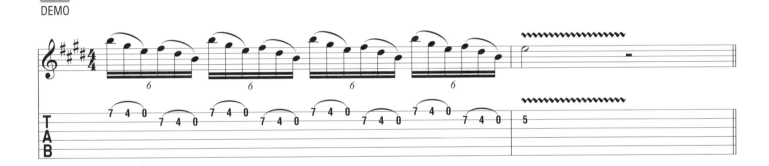

Move the shape down a few frets, and it can work in A major:

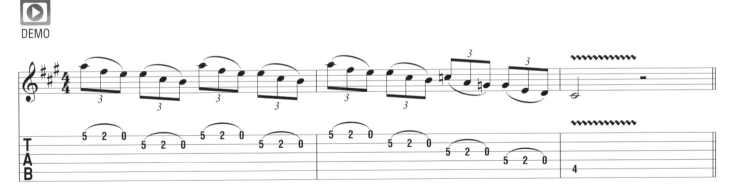

Again, some of these notes go out of key, or they come from the parallel major or minor scale, but that just adds to the character. As long as you resolve the lick well, you have a good amount of leeway in this regard.

Here's a good example of making some dissonance work for you. You can play this lick over a B chord that resolves to an E chord. That dissonant open G string gets resolved to the E chord's major 3rd, G#, at fret 1.

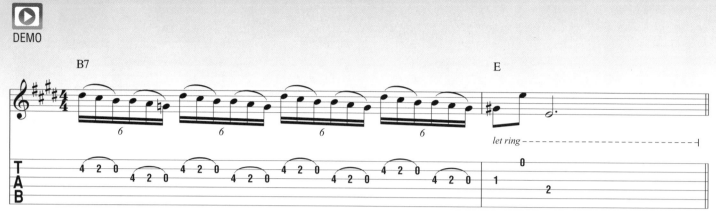

SCALE-FORM APPROACH

Another take on this idea is to conform to a scale pattern as you progress through the strings. For example, you could start with this G minor pentatonic form in third position:

G Minor Pentatonic

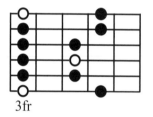

Then you could work down through the strings, pulling off each two-note fragment to the open string, like this:

Or, how about this A major pentatonic form in second position?

A Major Pentatonic – Second Position

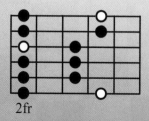

30

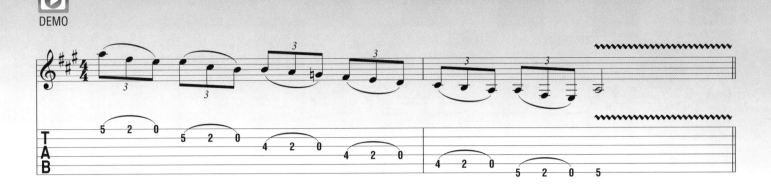

Or move up to A minor pentatonic in fifth position to get some wider intervals.

A Minor Pentatonic – Box Form

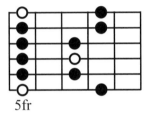

5fr

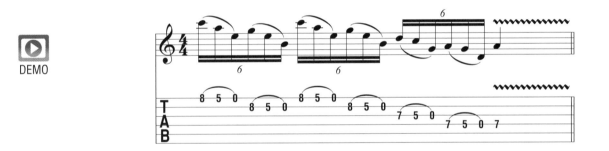

HORIZONTAL APPROACH

You can also work along the length of one string (or two), moving up through the scale horizontally. This is also a great way to familiarize yourself with the entire neck.

For example, if we lay out the notes of A minor pentatonic along string 3, it looks like this:

A Minor Pentatonic – Third String

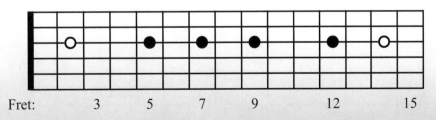

Fret: 3   5   7   9   12   15

So, we could work our way up through the scale by using a sequence of pull-offs, like this:

DEMO

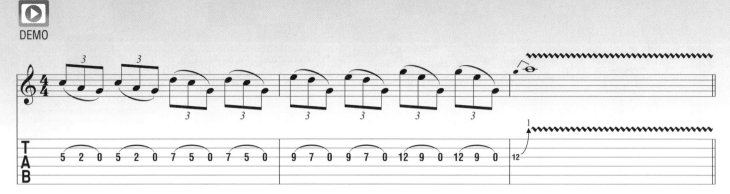

Or, how about the E minor pentatonic scale along the B string?

E Minor Pentatonic – Second String

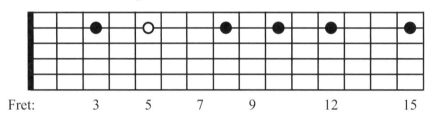

DEMO

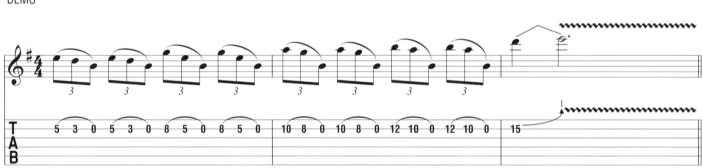

And again, the open string doesn't have to belong to the pentatonic scale you're using. Here's what the G minor pentatonic scale looks like on string 1:

G Minor Pentatonic – First String

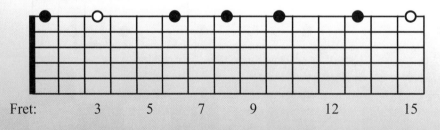

Notice that the open E string is not part of the scale, but it still sounds great within the lick.

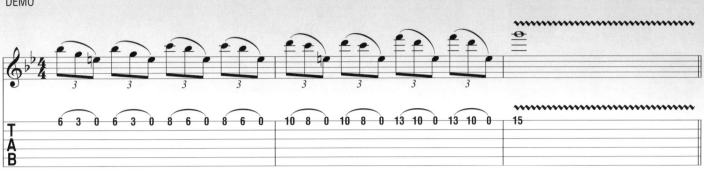

CHROMATIC HORIZONTAL APPROACH

And of course, there's simply the chromatic approach for sheer effect. Just take a shape, aim for a target note, and count the frets so that you end where you want to, on the right beat!

Key of E Minor (Targeting E Note)

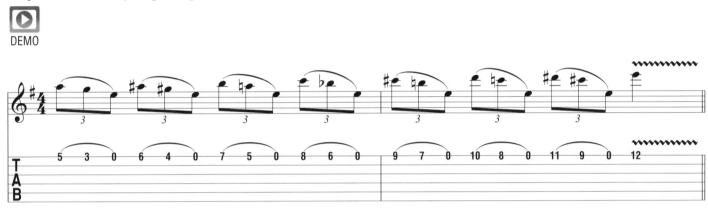

Key of A Minor (Targeting E Note)

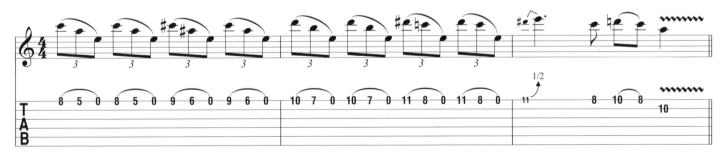

Key of G Minor (Targeting G Note)

Of course, you don't always have to move one fret at a time in one direction, either.

Key of D Minor (Targeting C Note)

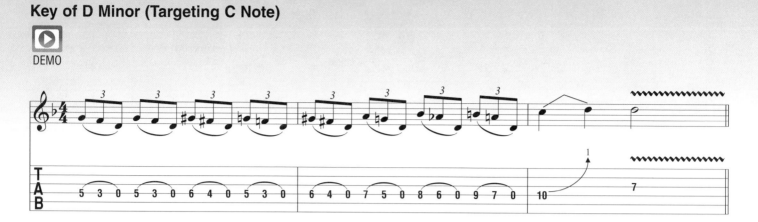

6ths

Using 6ths is another great way to build some texture and excitement in your solos. You hear them used all the time in country, rock 'n' roll, and soul music.

A Quick Bit of Background

If you're unfamiliar with this term, a "6th" refers to a music *interval*—or the musical distance between two notes. Simply put, you count note names to figure out the interval.

For example, from A to F is a 6th. How do we know? Just count the note names: A (1) – B (2) – C (3) – D (4) – E (5) – F (6).

From E to C is also a 6th: E (1) – F (2) – G (3) – A (4) – B (5) – C (6).

There are two types of 6th intervals you normally see: a major 6th and a minor 6th. The major 6th is one half step larger than the minor 6th.

6th Shapes

On the fretboard, 6ths are usually played on non-adjacent strings and occur in two different shapes, depending on which string sets are involved. Here are the major 6th shapes on each set of strings:

Major 6ths

The minor 6th shapes are simply one fret lower.

Minor 6ths

Thinking Horizontally

In order to use these 6th shapes, you need to see your scales in a horizontal fashion, similar to what we looked at on page 31. You're basically harmonizing a scale in 6th intervals; that is, you're playing the notes of a scale along two strings simultaneously.

Let's start with the G major scale, playing it in 6ths along strings 3 and 1.

G Major Scale in 6ths: Strings 3 and 1

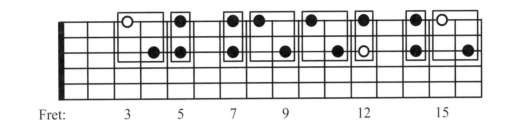

So, we're playing the notes of the G major scale—G, A, B, C, D, E, and F#—from G to G on string 1 and from B to B on string 3. Notice how we have a mix of major and minor 6th intervals to accommodate the scale steps.

Let's check out the A major scale—A, B, C#, D, E, F#, and G#—in 6ths on strings 4 and 2.

A Major Scale in 6ths: Strings 4 and 2

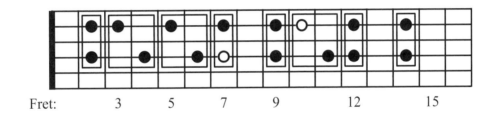

And here's one more: the C major scale—C, D, E, F, G, A, and B—on strings 3 and 1.

C Major Scale in 6ths: Strings 3 and 1

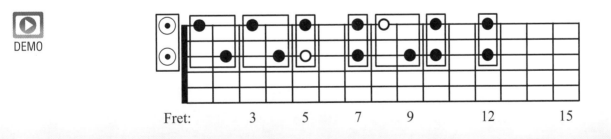

When using 6ths in solos, you'll find that the 3–1 string set is the most common.

6th Licks

Now let's check out what we can do with these shapes. Here's a lick in G that moves from a G chord to a C chord:

DEMO

And here's another great idea: using chromatic neighbor tones. You slide up to the lower note from a half step below.

DEMO

You can also use chromatic passing tones to fill in the gaps between two scale tones. Here's an example of that idea over a C chord:

DEMO

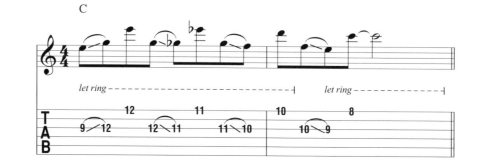

Here, we're using a chromatic passing tone to move from an A chord to a D chord:

DEMO

In "California Man," the solo climaxes with an ascending 6ths lick over F# and B chords:

California Man – 6ths

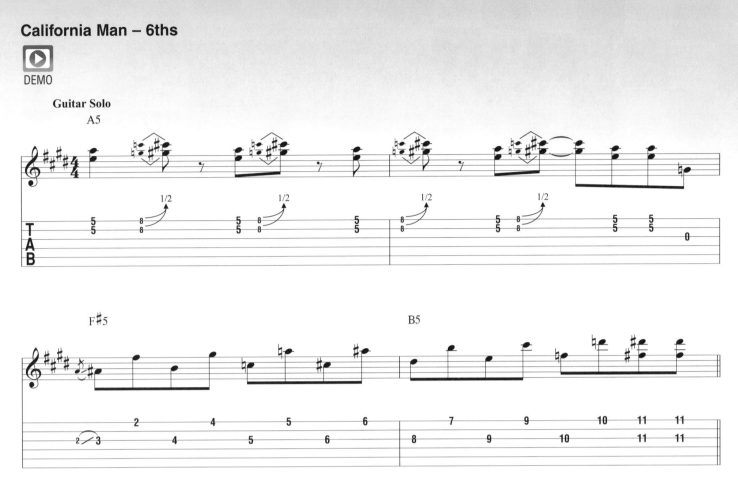

Strumming 6ths

In the licks we've played so far, each note was individually picked, but sometimes you'll want to strum a 6th interval to really lay into it. When you do that, you have to use a good amount of fret-hand muting to make sure that only the notes you want to sound are actually heard.

For example, if I want to strum the following B/G 6th interval on strings 3 and 1, I'm going to make sure that string 2 is touched by my index finger (on string 1) and/or my middle finger (on string 3) to keep it quiet. I'll also make sure to touch string 4 with the tip of my middle finger to deaden it.

If I *really* want to dig in and strum with wild abandon, I'll bring my thumb over the neck to also quiet strings 6 and 5.

By doing this, you can strum away and be sure that you're only hearing the notes you want to hear.

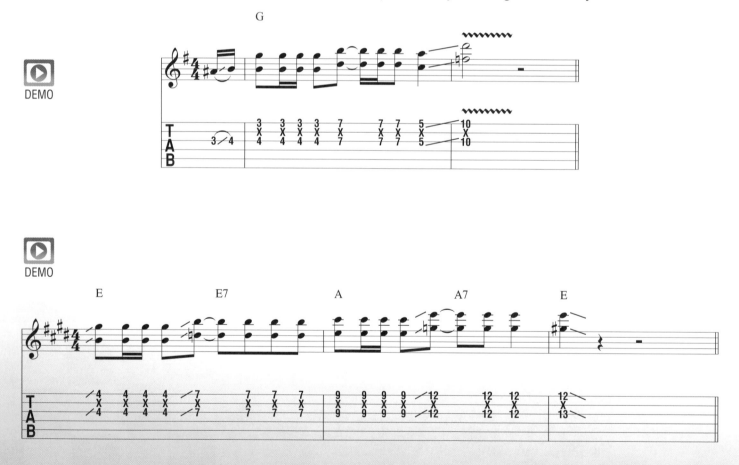

Rick's thoughts on keeping it simple

CHEAP RIFFS

A good riff can make a whole song. You may not remember all the words or all the licks in a solo, but if it's got a catchy riff, chances are, that'll stick with you. So in this section, we're going to look at riff-building and how it's done. It doesn't have to be complicated!

Keeping It Simple: The Power of Repetition

We like to recognize things when we listen to music. Whether it's a repeating lick in a solo or a chorus refrain that comes back around, when we hear something again, it helps us connect to the music. So, this is perhaps the #1 lesson in riff-building: *keep it simple* and exploit the *power of repetition*. Simply put, if it sounds good, do it again!

Based off an A chord, here's an example that works with some double stops in a catchy rhythm:

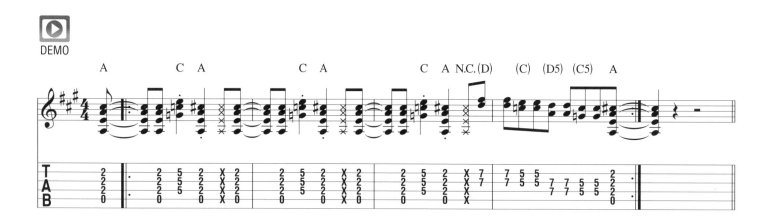

And here's one in E that adds a little twist to a common boogie pattern. Sometimes that's all it takes.

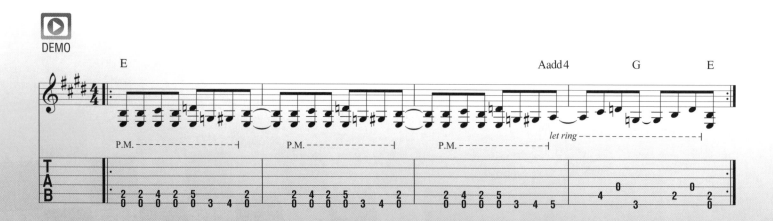

Of course, you don't have to repeat one chord or one riff over and over (although that can also be effective in the right context). Sometimes repetition means that you don't have to generate *entirely new material* all the time. Instead you can slightly alter one riff to function over a different chord, for example, or you can maybe change chords to make the same riff sound fresh again, etc. These are great strategies for getting the most out of what you have. And they still focus on the importance of using repetition to connect with the listener.

Let's check out some examples to hear these ideas in action. This first one's in A and transposes the same idea to A, D, and E chords.

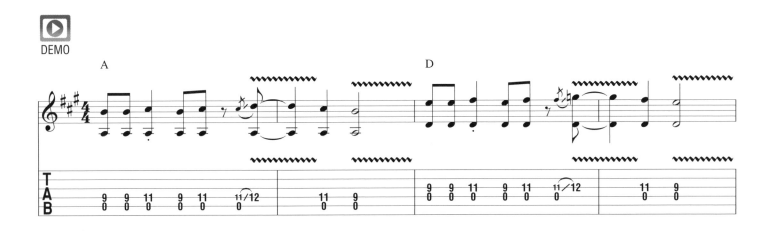

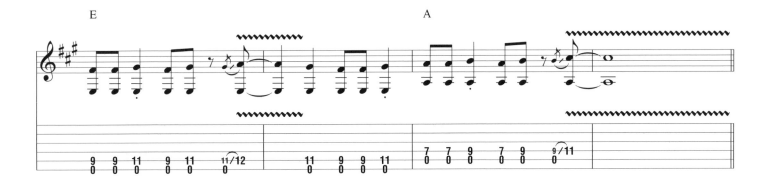

And here's one in C that transposes a power-chord-based figure to C5, G5, and F5 chords.

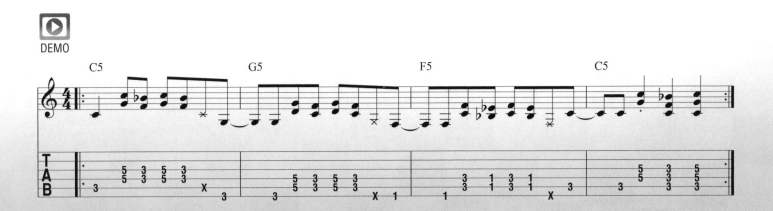

Here's another take, this time based off power-chord shapes and variations in E:

You can do the same kind of idea with open power-chord shapes, as well. This one uses open D, A, and G shapes:

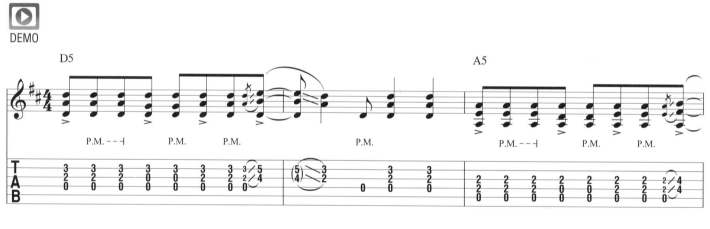

All of these riffs have a few things in common: repetition and the reuse/transposition of material.

Chord Variations: Sus Chords

A great way to liven up a chord riff is by slightly varying the chord to create a sense of movement. The *sus* chord (suspended chord) is extremely useful for this type of thing. Just ask Pete Townshend!

Sus Chord Types

There are several different types of sus chords, but we'll be working with two of the most common here: the sus2 and the sus4. In each of these types, the 3rd of the chord (major or minor) is replaced with a 2nd (sus2) or 4th (sus4). Consequently, the major or minor quality of the chord is "suspended." This is to say that sus chords are neither major nor minor because the 3rd—the defining note in a major or minor triad—is not present.

Here are some common open chords and their sus4 and/or sus2 counterparts:

D

132

Dsus2
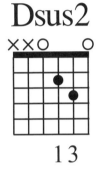

13

Dsus4
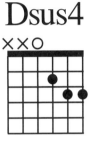

134

A
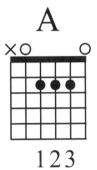

123

Asus2
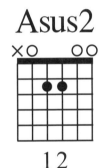

12

Asus4
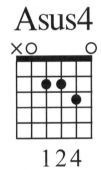

124

C
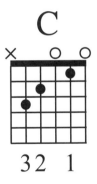

32 1

Csus2
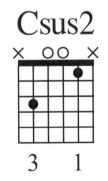

3   1

Csus4

34 1

F
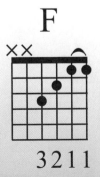

3211

Fsus2
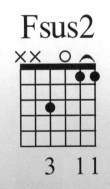

3 11

Fsus4

3411

For E and G chords, only the sus4 is commonly used in open position.

E
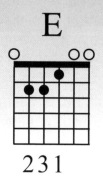
2 3 1

Esus4
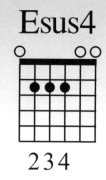
2 3 4

G
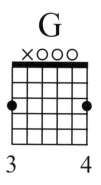
3   4

Gsus4
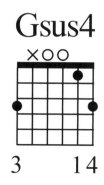
3   1 4

Sus Chord Riffs

Let's put some of these to use in some riffs.

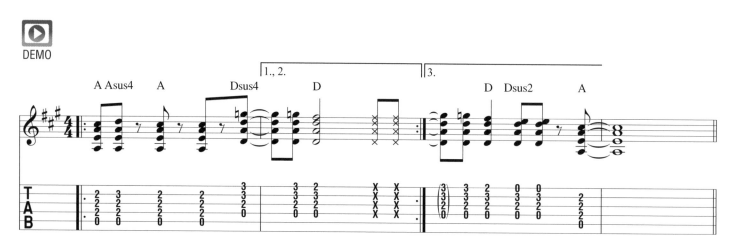

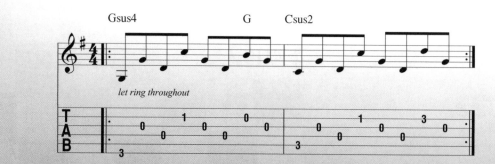

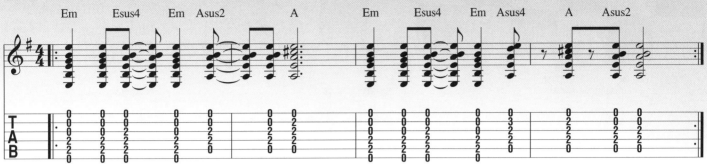

We can create moveable barre forms of these chords for playing in other keys, as well. The most common are the E-form and A-form shapes.

For the E-form shape, you can grab a bass note on string 6 with your thumb to add some extra bottom. The F chords we looked at earlier are E-form chords, only they didn't have the low bass note.

Rick's thoughts on using the thumb

Here's a way to play E-form G and Gsus4 chords:

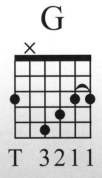

G

T 3211

Gsus4

T 3411

For the A-form shape, you can either barre strings 4-2 with your ring finger (some people use their pinky instead), or you can use a 2-3-4 fingering. With the A-form shape, we can get both the sus2 and the sus4 chords:

Let's check out these forms in some riffs.

You can hear A-form sus chords—both open Asus2 and the moveable forms for Bsus4 and Bsus2—in the intro riff to "The Flame."

The Flame – Sus Chords

Chord Variations: Changing Bass Notes

Another great strategy for creating a sense of movement in chordal riffs is to experiment with changing bass notes. There aren't really any strict rules for this approach, so feel free to explore.

Simply take a chord and try moving the bass note around a bit to see what you get. Take a Dsus2 chord, for example. You may come up with something like the example below. Don't worry too much about the strange chord names. If it sounds good, it is good!

Or take an A chord and put some different bass notes beneath it:

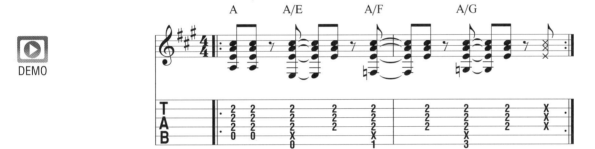

You can even get creative with two-note power-chord shapes. Move the bass notes around to see what happens!

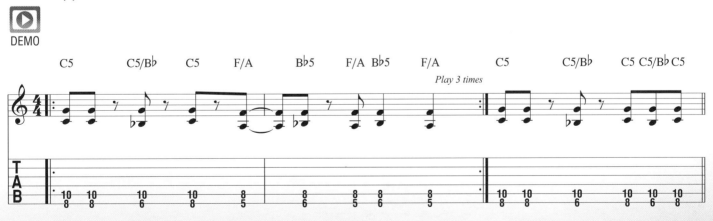

In "If You Want My Love," you can see this strategy applied in the pre-chorus, where the same descending-bass-line move appears in three different chords: Em, Am, and Dm.

If You Want My Love – Changing Bass Notes

DEMO

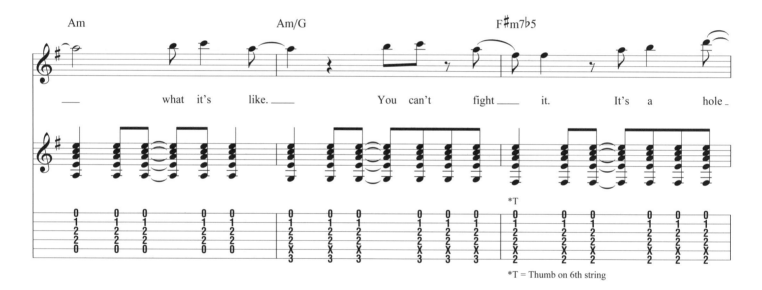

*T = Thumb on 6th string

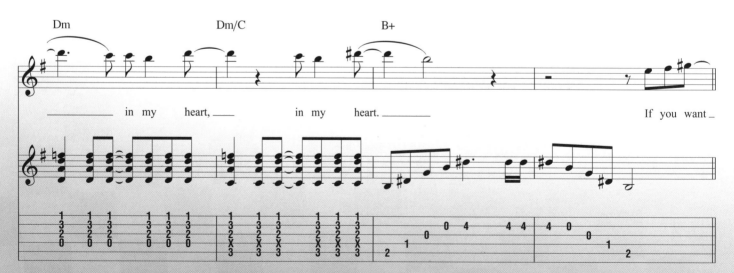

Using Chromatics

Another great way to energize a song and create some well-needed tension now and then is by using *chromatics*. By this, we simply mean moving chords or notes by a half step (one fret). As with changing bass notes, there are really no rules for this type of thing; you just find a spot that needs a little excitement and try some things out!

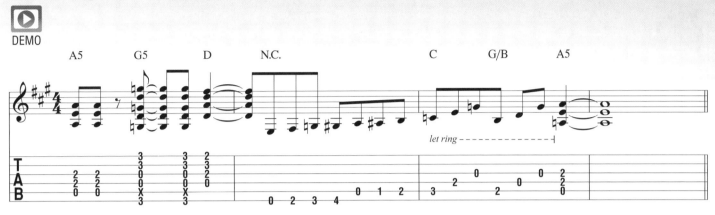

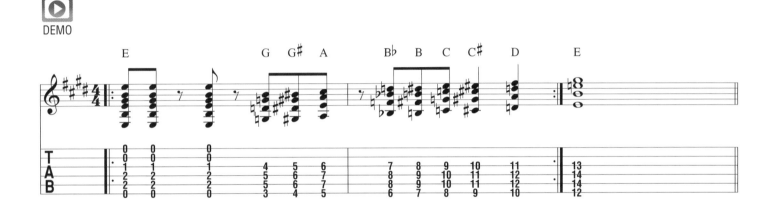

You can also combine two approaches. Here's a chromatic take on the changing-bass-notes approach:

Another idea is to have one voice within a chord or riff moving chromatically. Here's a progression in C demonstrating that:

And here's how you might apply this concept to a riff in A:

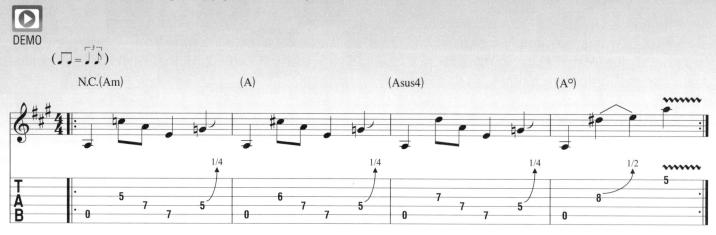

In "Dream Police," the interlude kicks off with a chromatic move over a B chord that creates a nice, dramatic progression.

Dream Police – Chromatics

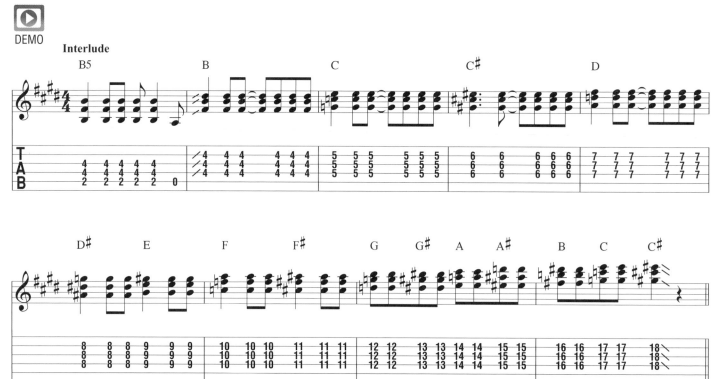

Octaves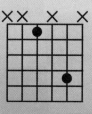

A simple way to strengthen a riff or make it stand out a bit is to use *octaves*. This is equally effective in solos or rhythm parts, and it's also great for doubling vocal lines. You'll hear octaves used by everyone from Hendrix to Van Halen and countless players in between. Let's have a look at how it's done.

Octave Shapes

The most common octave shapes are played on string sets 6-4, 5-3, 4-2, and 3-1. In other words, you'll have an in-between string that you'll need to keep quiet—when you're strumming the shapes, that is. Notice that, when the second string is involved or crossed over, the shape spans three frets instead of two.

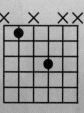 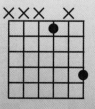

The fret-hand technique for playing octaves is essentially the same as for 6th intervals (see page 34). You'll need to use fret-hand muting to keep the unwanted strings from ringing. For example, to play the following third-position C octave shape on strings 5 and 3, you'll need to do the following:

- Deaden string 6 with the tip of your index finger
- Deaden string 4 with the pad of your index finger and/or the tip of your ring (or pinky) finger
- Deaden string 2 with the tip of your ring (or pinky) finger
- Deaden strings 2 and 1 with the underside of your index finger

A little redundancy—that is, two different ways of muting one string—is never a bad thing when it comes to fret-hand muting.

Octave Riffs

Now let's check out some examples. Here's one in A that uses chords and octaves in a call-and-response fashion:

DEMO

In this G minor riff, you can imagine the whole band joining in for an anthem-like octave phrase:

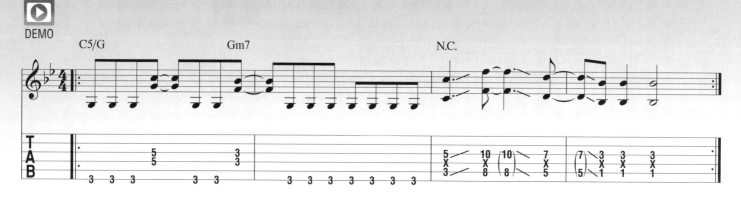

Octaves are used exclusively in the guitar solo of "If You Want My Love," essentially restating the vocal hook in all its glory.

If You Want My Love – Octaves

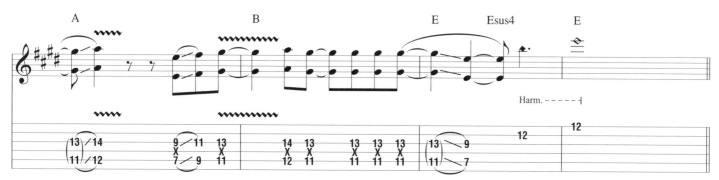

Rick's thoughts on the toggle switch trick

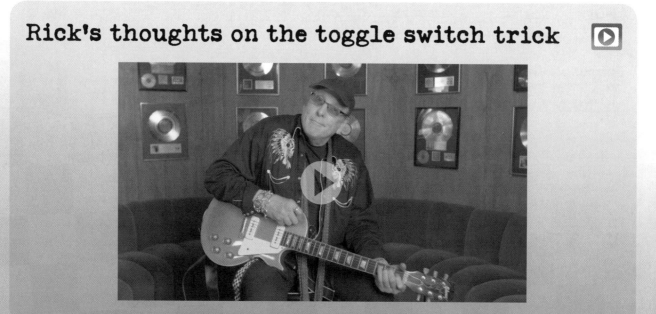

APPENDIX

More Videos

Be sure to check out more videos from Rick, including a look at his famous guitar collection!

- ### Influences and Anecdotes
  Rick discusses his favorite guitarists and shares many fun stories from his long career in rock 'n' roll.

- ### Bonus Material
  Take an exclusive look at some of the coolest guitars in Rick Nielsen's collection.

- ### Outtakes
  Hilarious clips and bloopers from the video shoot!

Scale Forms

Here, you'll find all the scale forms covered in this book, as well as a few others. These are all presented in the key of A, but they can all be transposed by sliding them up or down the neck to a new tonic.

A Minor Pentatonic – Form 1

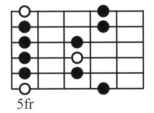

5fr

A Minor Pentatonic – Form 2

Extension box

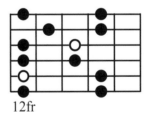

7fr

A Minor Pentatonic – Form 3

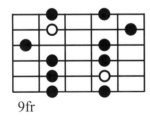

9fr

A Minor Pentatonic – Form 4

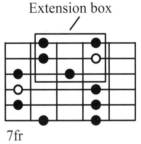

12fr

A Minor Pentatonic – Form 5

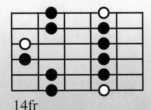

14fr

A Blues Scale – Form 1

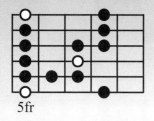

5fr

A Blues Scale – Form 2

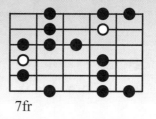

7fr

A Blues Scale – Form 3

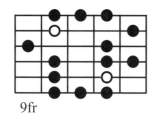

9fr

A Blues Scale – Form 4

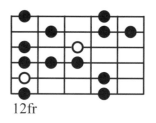

12fr

A Blues Scale – Form 5

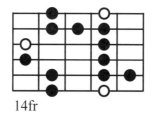

14fr

A Major Pentatonic – Form 1

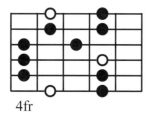

4fr

A Major Pentatonic – Form 2

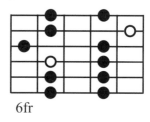

6fr

A Major Pentatonic – Form 3

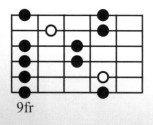

9fr

A Major Pentatonic – Form 4

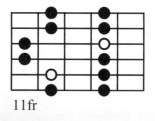

11fr

A Major Pentatonic – Form 5

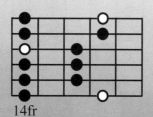

14fr

Chord Forms

Here are all the chord forms we looked at throughout the book, as well as a few others. Remember that any chord that doesn't include an open string is a moveable form and can be played from any root by moving it up or down the neck.

D	Dsus2	Dsus4	A	Asus2	Asus4
	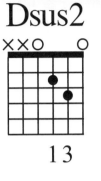		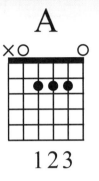		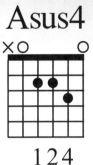
1 3 2	1 3	1 3 4	1 2 3	1 2	1 2 4

C	Csus2	Csus4	F	Fsus2
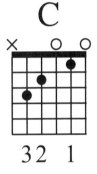	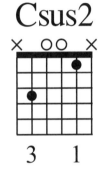	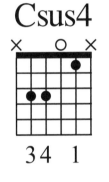	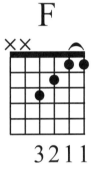	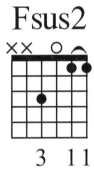
3 2 1	3 1	3 4 1	3 2 1 1	3 1 1

Fsus4	E	Esus4	G	Gsus4
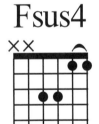		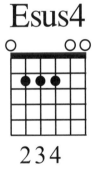	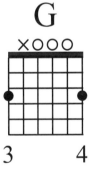	
3 4 1 1	2 3 1	2 3 4	3 4	3 1 4

G	Gsus4	B	Bsus2	Bsus4
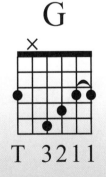		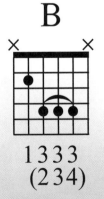		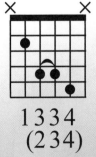
T 3 2 1 1	T 3 4 1 1	1 3 3 3 (2 3 4)	1 3 4 1 1	1 3 3 4 (2 3 4)

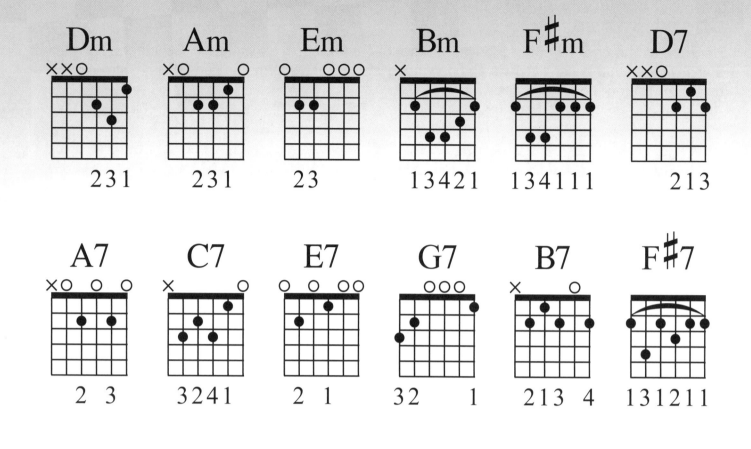